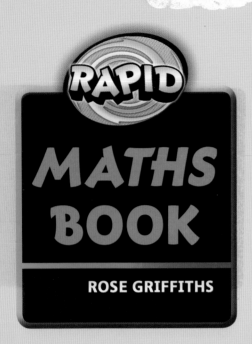

RAPID

MATHS BOOK

ROSE GRIFFITHS

Heinemann

Heinemann is an imprint of Pearson Education Limited, a company incorporated in England and Wales, having its registered office at Edinburgh Gate, Harlow, Essex, CM20 2JE. Registered company number: 872828

www.heinemann.co.uk

Heinemann is a registered trademark of Pearson Education Limited

Text © Rose Griffiths 1996, 2005, 2009

First published 1996
Second edition first published 2005
Third edition first published 2009

13 12
10 9 8 7 6 5 4 3

British Library Cataloguing in Publication Data
A catalogue record for this book is available from the British Library.

ISBN 978 0 435912 33 8

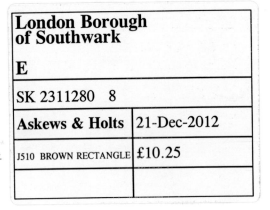
Designed and produced by Debbie Oatley @ room9design
Original illustrations © Pearson Education Ltd 2009
Illustrated by Bill Ledger, Matt Latchford, Pet Gotohda and Matt Buckley
Cover illustration © Pearson Education Ltd
Cover illustration by Matt Latchford
Printed in Malaysia, CTP-PJB

Acknowledgements
We would like to thank St Gilberts C of E Primary School, Stamford for their invaluable help in the development and trialling of this course.

The author and publisher would like to thank the following individuals and organisations for permission to reproduce photographs:

©Shutterstock / marymary: p. 34 (buttons); ©Brand X Pictures: p. 35 (pencil case 2); ©Shutterstock / Jeff Gynane: p. 35 (pencil case 3); ©Shutterstock / Paula Danielse: p. 35 (pencil case 4); ©Shutterstock / bart 78: p. 35 (pencil case 5); ©Shutterstock / Kschrei: p. 35 (apples). All other photos © Pearson Education / Clark Wiseman, Studio 8.

Every effort has been made to contact copyright holders of material reproduced in this book. Any omissions will be rectified in subsequent printings if notice is given to the publishers.

Websites
The websites used in this book were correct and up-to-date at the time of publication. It is essential for tutors to preview each website before using it in class so as to ensure that the URL is still accurate, relevant and appropriate. We suggest that tutors bookmark useful websites and consider enabling students to access them through the school/college intranet.

Contents

Using this book   4

Part 1   7

Counting to 150
Using money
Addition and subtraction within 80
Mental recall of tables facts: all of the 0, 1, 2 and 10 times tables,
    and 3s, 4s and 5s within 25
Ordinal numbers (1st to 31st)
$\frac{1}{2}$s and $\frac{1}{4}$s
Multiplying 2-digit numbers by 2 or 3 within 80

Part 2   37

Counting to 180
Using money
Addition and subtraction within 100
Mental recall of tables facts: all of the 0, 1, 2, 3, 4, 5 and
    10 times tables
Multiples of 6 to 60
Multiplying by 2, 3, 4 and 5 within 100
Dividing by 2 within 100
Negative numbers

Part 3   67

Counting to 200
Using money
Addition and subtraction within 120
Mental recall of tables facts: all of the 0, 1, 2, 3,
    4, 5 and 10 times tables, **and** 6s within 36
Mental recall of number bonds within 20
Multiplying and dividing by 2, 3, 5 and 10 within 120
$\frac{1}{2}$s, $\frac{1}{4}$s, $\frac{1}{3}$s and $\frac{1}{5}$s

Using this book

Welcome to *Rapid Maths*.

Your teacher will talk to you about where you will start in *Rapid Maths*.

Getting started

Check that you can do the first two pages in each part of this book, before you do any more.

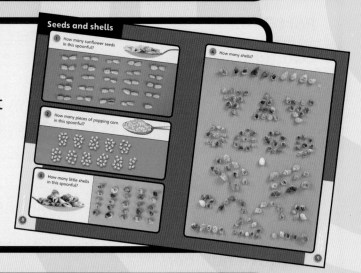

Reading

There are word lists in the Teacher's Guide.

These will help you learn any new words you need.

I've made cards from my list.

Extra activities

There are more activities and games in the Copymasters, Games Pack and Home Maths Book.

There is Practice Software too, with activities for each level of *Rapid Maths*.

> Take them home for extra practice!

> We like doing the Speedy Tables.

> Can we get more right, and get quicker?

Progress tests and Record sheets

These are in the Teacher's Guide.

> Check on your progress...

> and keep a record of what you've done!

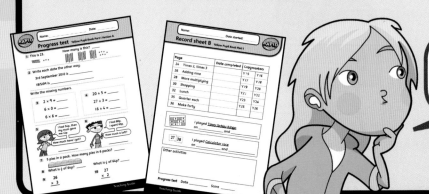

Part I
Contents

Seeds and shells	Counting to 150	8
Months and years	Writing dates	10
Off by heart	Mental recall of tables facts within 25	12
Add or take away	Addition and subtraction within 80	14
Days and dates	Understanding a calendar	16
Speedy tables	Mental recall of tables facts	18
Squares	Square numbers within 36	20
Ways of adding	Addition within 80	22
Times 2, times 3	Multiplication within 80	24
Adding nine	Addition of 9 within 80	26
More multiplying	Multiplication within 80	28
Shopping	Using money	30
Lunch	Multiplication and division by 2, 3, 4 and 5	32
Quarter each	Finding a quarter of a group	34
Make forty	Combinations to make 40	36

Counting and place value

Addition and subtraction

Multiplication and division

Mixed problems

Seeds and shells

1 How many sunflower seeds in this spoonful?

2 How many pieces of popping corn in this spoonful?

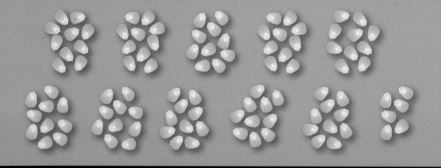

3 How many little shells in this spoonful?

Months and years

Write question numbers 1 to 12.
Ask your partner to read these months to you.
Write them down.

1	January	5	May	9	September
2	February	6	June	10	October
3	March	7	July	11	November
4	April	8	August	12	December

Ask your partner to check your spelling. ✔ or ✗

Now <u>you</u> read the months to your partner.

1st is the short way of writing First .

2nd → second   3rd → third   4th → fourth

Copy and complete.

13 1st, 2nd, 3rd, 4th, 5th, 6th, 7th, 8th, 9th, 10th, 11th

14 12th, 13th, 14th, 15th, 16th, 17th, 18th, 19th, 20th, 21st

15 22nd, ___, ___, ___, ___, 27th, ___, 29th, ___, ___

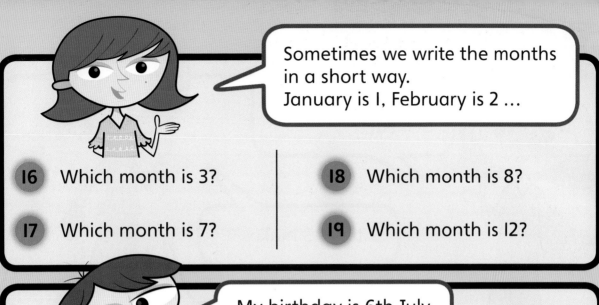

Sometimes we write the months in a short way.
January is 1, February is 2 ...

16 Which month is 3?

18 Which month is 8?

17 Which month is 7?

19 Which month is 12?

My birthday is 6th July.

My date of birth is 6th July 1972.
6 / 7 / 72

20 When is your birthday?

21 What is your date of birth? Write it both ways.

Write these dates of birth in numbers.

22 5th May 1955

23 6th June 1966

24 4th April 1944

25 7th July 1977

26 What is special about our dates of birth?

27 Which of us is the oldest?

Off by heart

Which tables facts do you know off by heart?

2 times 3 makes 6.

8 divided by 2 makes 4.

If you work out a tables fact lots of times, you can learn the answer off by heart.

Copy and complete.

Ring any you know off by heart.

Off by heart
1. 2 × 2 = 4
2. 4 × 3 =

1	2 × 2	6	8 ÷ 4	11	4 × 4
2	4 × 3	7	6 ÷ 2	12	1 × 4
3	1 × 3	8	12 ÷ 3	13	0 × 3
4	2 × 4	9	6 ÷ 3	14	1 × 2
5	4 × 0	10	0 ÷ 3	15	3 × 3

What's 4 × 5?

I'll work it out. 5, 10, 15, 20. It's 20.

Practise your tables until you know them off by heart.
Copy and complete.

16	3 × 5	18	10 ÷ 5	20	2 × 5
17	5 × 4	19	20 ÷ 5	21	5 × 5

Do these make 0?
Write <u>Yes</u> or <u>No</u>.

Check

22	0 × 5	24	0 × 0	26	4 × 0
23	3 × 0	25	1 × 0	27	0 × 567

Do these make 2?
Write <u>Yes</u> or <u>No</u>.

28	0 × 2	30	1 × 1	32	2 × 2
29	1 × 2	31	2 × 1	33	2 × 0

Ask if you can play 'Times tables bingo'.

Ⓖ

Mental recall of tables facts within 25
Copymaster Y4 and 'Times tables bingo'
(Y27 and Y28)

9 marbles in the tin.

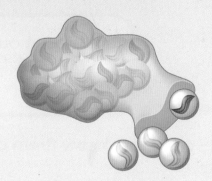
32 in the bag.

$$32 + 9 = 41$$

41 altogether.

Write each sum and work it out.

1

43 stickers in the book.

28 stickers here. →

How many altogether?

2

I had 72p.
I spent 25p.

How much is left?

3

← 24 pencils here.

39 pencils here. →

How many altogether?

4 7 badges here.

47 badges in the box.

How many altogether?

5 36 photos were on this camera. Then I deleted 18.

How many photos are left?

6 I had 80p. I spent 53p.

How much is left?

7 I had 68p, then my mum gave me 10p. How much have I got?

8 I've got 46p

I've got 25p more than you. How much have I got?

q I'm 13 years old.

I'm 47 years older than you.

How old am I?

Addition and subtraction within 80
Copymasters Y5 and Y6

Days and dates

Write question numbers 1 to 7.
Ask your partner to read the days to you. Write them down.

1	Monday	**4**	Thursday	**6**	Saturday
2	Tuesday	**5**	Friday	**7**	Sunday
3	Wednesday				

Ask your partner to check your spelling. ✔ or ✗

Now <u>you</u> read the days to your partner.

8 Which day do <u>you</u> think is the hardest to spell?

9 What is the day after Monday?

10 What is the day after Friday?

11 What is the day after Sunday?

12 How many days are there in one week?

How many days in:

13 2 weeks?   **15** 4 weeks?

14 3 weeks?   **16** 5 weeks?

17

How many days in a fortnight?

How many days in each month?

18 Copy this.

Thirty days in September,

April, June and November,

All the rest have thirty-one,

Except February, with twenty-eight days clear

And twenty-nine in each leap year.

JULY 2009

M	T	W	T	F	S	S
		1	2	3	4	5
6	7	8	9	10	11	12
13	14	15	16	17	18	19
20	21	22	23	24	25	26
27	28	29	30	31		

AUGUST 2009

M	T	W	T	F	S	S
					1	2
3	4	5	6	7	8	9
10	11	12	13	14	15	16
17	18	19	20	21	22	23
24	25	26	27	28	29	30
31						

1st July 2009 is a <u>Wednesday</u>.

19 Which day is 31st July 2009?

20 Which day is 1st August 2009?

Work with a partner. Use a calendar for this year.
Take it in turns to ask each other questions like these.

Which <u>day</u> is September 10th?

What <u>date</u> is the first Monday in June?

Work with a partner.

Write question numbers 1 to 20.
Ask your partner to read the questions to you.

**Write your answers
as quickly as you can.**

1	1 × 2	**8**	90 ÷ 10	**15**	5 × 5		
2	3 × 5	**9**	6 ÷ 6	**16**	15 ÷ 5		
3	4 × 3	**10**	20 ÷ 4	**17**	2 × 3		
4	10 × 7	**11**	8 ÷ 2	**18**	30 ÷ 10		
5	5 × 4	**12**	7 ÷ 1	**19**	0 × 5		
6	1 × 1	**13**	16 ÷ 4	**20**	18 ÷ 2		
7	3 × 3	**14**	12 ÷ 3				

 ✔ or ✘

**Now <u>you</u> read the questions
to your partner.**

Mental recall of tables facts

How many 2s make 16?

2s into 16 ... that's 8.

21	$16 \div 2$	24	$9 \div 3$	27	$25 \div 5$
22	$3 \div 1$	25	$8 \div 4$	28	$5 \div 5$
23	$20 \div 10$	26	$40 \div 10$	29	$5 \div 1$

Copy and complete.

30 $\boxed{4} \times 3 = 12$

31 $\boxed{4} \times 5 = 20$

32 $2 \times \boxed{7} = 14$

33 $10 \times \boxed{10} = 100$

34 $\boxed{9} \times 1 = 9$

35 $8 \times \boxed{0} = 0$

Use a stopwatch or a sand timer.

Use Speedy tables A made from Copymaster Y10.

Can you get 20 questions right in 3 minutes?

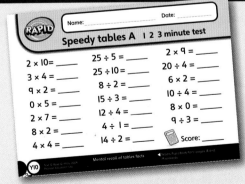

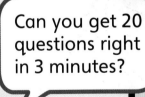

Check your answers. ✔ or ✘
Count how many you got right.

Ask what to do next.

Squares

1 row of 1 brick

$1 \times 1 = 1$

2 rows of 2 bricks

$2 \times 2 = 4$

3 rows of 3 bricks

1 How many altogether?

2 $3 \times 3 = 9$

4 rows of 4 bricks

3 How many altogether?

4 $4 \times 4 = 16$

These bricks are in a square.
Each side measures
the same amount.

You can make a square
with 9 bricks.

9 is called a <u>square number</u>.

5 Use 12 bricks. Can you make a square with them?

No spaces allowed!

---

6 How many red bricks in this square?

7 How many blue bricks?

8 How many bricks altogether?

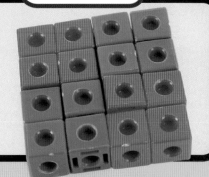

---

9 How many red bricks in this square?

10 How many blue bricks?

11 How many bricks altogether?

---

12 How many red bricks in this square?

13 How many blue bricks?

14 How many bricks altogether?

---

15 Use 25 bricks. Can you make a square?

16 Use 30 bricks. Can you make a square?

17 Use 36 bricks. Can you make a square?

Ways of adding

What is the <u>best</u> way of adding?

There are lots of good ways.

Do these in your head.

1	10 + 10	**5**	11 + 50	**9**	40 + 20
2	9 + 30	**6**	12 + 3	**10**	29 + 3
3	5 + 7	**7**	8 + 8	**11**	20 + 9
4	64 + 2	**8**	25 + 25	**12**	65 + 5

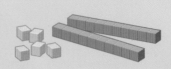

Do these with tens and ones.

13	25 + 54	**17**	41 + 26	**21**	51 + 25
14	18 + 47	**18**	17 + 17	**22**	8 + 45
15	62 + 18	**19**	40 + 37		
16	35 + 37	**20**	32 + 44		

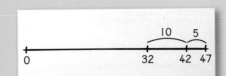

Do these on paper.

23	32 + 15	**26**	61 + 7	**29**	29 + 45
24	26 + 41	**27**	13 + 52	**30**	42 + 26
25	35 + 36	**28**	46 + 30	**31**	35 + 35

Do these with a calculator.

32	37 + 37	**35**	21 + 49	**38**	36 + 25
33	16 + 53	**36**	28 + 27	**39**	43 + 39
34	25 + 39	**37**	19 + 19	**40**	49 + 14

Do these sums. Write how you did them.

41 30 + 25

42 47 + 28

Ask if you can play the 'Calculator race' game.

Addition within 80
Copymasters Y13 and Y14
The 'Calculator race' game (Y29 and Y30)

Times 2, times 3

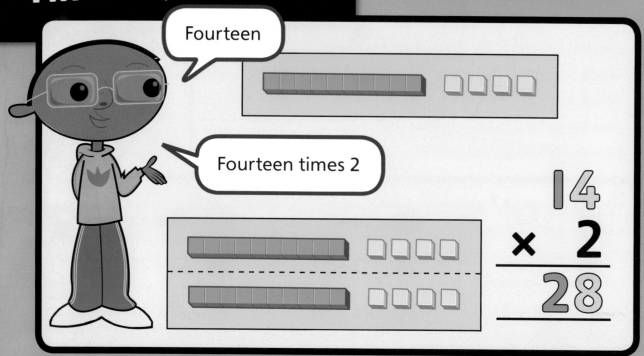

Fourteen

Fourteen times 2

$$14 \times 2 = 28$$

Make two lots of each number with tens and ones.

Copy and complete.

Thirteen	**1** $\begin{array}{r} 13 \\ \times\ 2 \\ \hline 26 \end{array}$
Twenty-one	**2** $\begin{array}{r} 21 \\ \times\ 2 \\ \hline 42 \end{array}$
Twenty-four	**3** $\begin{array}{r} 24 \\ \times\ 2 \\ \hline 48 \end{array}$
Thirty-three	**4** $\begin{array}{r} 33 \\ \times\ 2 \\ \hline 66 \end{array}$ ✔ or ✗

20 times 2 is 40.
So 23 times 2
will be <u>more</u> than 40.

23×2

$$\begin{array}{r} 23 \\ \times\ 2 \\ \hline 46 \end{array}$$

$20 \times 2 = 40$

$3 \times 2 = 6$

Use tens and ones. Copy and complete.

5
$$\begin{array}{r} 31 \\ \times\ 2 \\ \hline \end{array}$$

6
$$\begin{array}{r} 27 \\ \times\ 2 \\ \hline \end{array}$$

7
$$\begin{array}{r} 35 \\ \times\ 2 \\ \hline \end{array}$$

Now make three lots of each number.

8
$$\begin{array}{r} 11 \\ \times\ 3 \\ \hline \end{array}$$

10
$$\begin{array}{r} 15 \\ \times\ 3 \\ \hline \end{array}$$

12
$$\begin{array}{r} 16 \\ \times\ 3 \\ \hline \end{array}$$

14
$$\begin{array}{r} 12 \\ \times\ 3 \\ \hline \end{array}$$

9
$$\begin{array}{r} 20 \\ \times\ 3 \\ \hline \end{array}$$

11
$$\begin{array}{r} 22 \\ \times\ 3 \\ \hline \end{array}$$

13
$$\begin{array}{r} 24 \\ \times\ 3 \\ \hline \end{array}$$

15
$$\begin{array}{r} 25 \\ \times\ 3 \\ \hline \end{array}$$

Adding nine

1 How many here?

2 How many here?

Nine is <u>one less</u> than ten.

If you want to add 9, you can add 10, then 'go back' one.

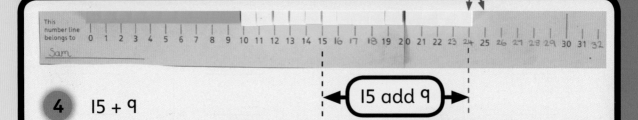

3 15 + 10

15 add 10

4 15 + 9

15 add 9

5 27 + 10	**7** 36 + 10	**9** 65 + 10
6 27 + 9	**8** 36 + 9	**10** 65 + 9

Add nine

A game for 2 or 3 people.
You need: cards numbered 1 to 70 and a calculator.

Shuffle the cards.

Put them in a pile, face down.

Take the top card.
Add nine to that number.

Your partner can check with a calculator.

If you are right, keep the card.
If not, put it back at the bottom of the pile.

Now it is your partner's turn.

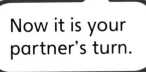

Have ten turns each <u>or</u> keep going until all the cards have gone.

Count how many cards you won.

Addition of 9 within 80
Copymasters Y17 and Y18

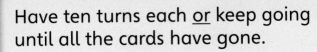

27

More multiplying

12 times 2

12 times 3

12 times 4

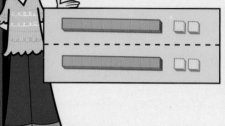

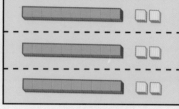

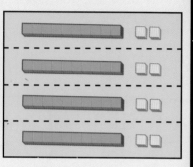

Copy and complete.

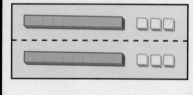

1
$$\begin{array}{r} 12 \\ \times \quad 2 \\ \hline \\ \hline \end{array}$$

2
$$\begin{array}{r} 12 \\ \times \quad 3 \\ \hline \\ \hline \end{array}$$

3
$$\begin{array}{r} 12 \\ \times \quad 4 \\ \hline \\ \hline \end{array}$$

13 times 2

13 times 3

13 times 4

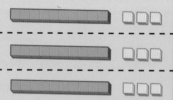

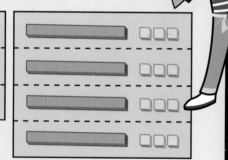

Copy and complete.

4
$$\begin{array}{r} 13 \\ \times \quad 2 \\ \hline 10 \\ \hline \end{array}$$

5
$$\begin{array}{r} 13 \\ \times \quad 3 \\ \hline 19 \\ \hline \end{array}$$

6
$$\begin{array}{r} 13 \\ \times \quad 4 \\ \hline 27 \\ \hline \end{array}$$

28

14 x 3

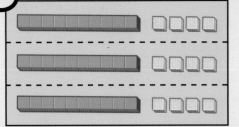

$$14 \times 3$$

$$42$$

10 x 3 = 30   4 x 3 = 12

30 + 12 = 42

When I multiply on paper, I write it like this:

$$14$$
$$\times 3$$
$$30 \quad (10 \times 3)$$
$$12 \quad (4 \times 3)$$
$$42$$

Use tens and ones. Then multiply on paper.

7
$$24$$
$$\times \quad 3$$
31

9
$$23$$
$$\times \quad 3$$
20

11
$$17$$
$$\times \quad 2$$
24

13
$$32$$
$$\times \quad 3$$

8
$$22$$
$$\times \quad 3$$

10
$$22$$
$$\times \quad 4$$

12
$$18$$
$$\times \quad 3$$

14
$$18$$
$$\times \quad 2$$

Multiplication within 80
Copymasters Y19 and Y20

Shopping

Use notes and coins.

I bought some jeans.

£12.99

1 How much change?

I bought a hat.

£7.50

2 How much change?

I bought a jumper.

£7.75

3 How much change?

I bought a pair of socks.

£1.99 a pair

4 How much change?

I bought a jumper.

£11.50

5 How much change?

T-shirt   £4·50

Shorts   £8·00

6   How much did I spend?

7   How much change from £15?

Gloves   £2·50

Jumper   £11·00

8   How much did I spend?

13·50

9   How much change from £20?

Socks   £1·50

T-shirt   £6·00

Jeans   £10·00

10   How much did I spend?

11   How much change from £20?

Hat   £7·50

Jumper   £12·50

12   How much did I spend?

13   How much change from £20?

3 drinks in a pack. How many in 2 packs?

3 times 2. That's 6.

3 drinks in a pack.
How many drinks in:

1 4 packs?

2 5 packs?

3 6 packs?

4 9 packs?

5 7 packs?

2 cakes in a pack. How many cakes in:

2 MUFFINS

6 2 packs?

7 5 packs?

8 6 packs?

9 8 packs?

10 7 packs?

11 10 packs?

12 How many cakes in 20 packs?

13 How many cakes in 25 packs?

4 soups in a pack.
How many soups in:

14 3 packs?

15 4 packs?

16 6 packs?

17 7 packs?

18 10 packs?

19 9 packs?

20 8 packs?

4 SOUPS

21

> How many soups in 15 packs?

> I don't like soup!

5 APPLE PIES

5 pies in a pack. How many pies in:

22 2 packs?

23 4 packs?

24 5 packs?

25 7 packs?

26 10 packs?

27 9 packs?

28

> How many pies in 12 packs?

29

> How many pies in 15 packs?

Multiplication and division by
2, 3, 4 and 5
Copymasters Y23 and Y24

We can share these.

A quarter each.

What is a quarter of 8?

| 8 | ÷ | 4 | = | 2 |

A quarter of 8 is 2.

---

1 What is a quarter of 12?

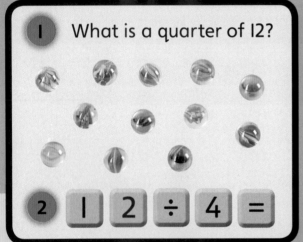

2 | 1 | 2 | ÷ | 4 | = |

3 What is a quarter of 16?

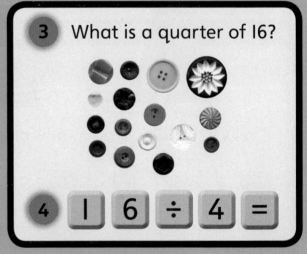

4 | 1 | 6 | ÷ | 4 | = |

---

5 What is a quarter of 20?

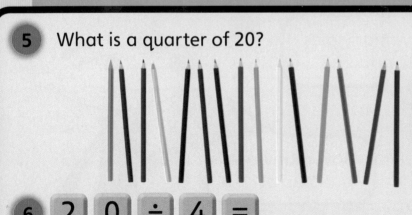

6 | 2 | 0 | ÷ | 4 | = |

7 What is a quarter of 4?

8 4 ÷ 4 =

Can you <u>always</u> have exactly a quarter each?

Talk to your teacher about these.

5 pencil cases

5 apples

9 Can I have a quarter of these?

10 Can I have a quarter of these?

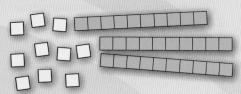

Find as many ways as you can to make 40.

You can add, take away, multiply or divide.

Write each way.

Make forty
20 × 2
10 + 10 + 10 + 10
50 − 10

Make sure they are all different.

Ask your partner to check.

 ✔ or ✘

Part 2
Contents

One hundred and eighty	Counting to 180	38
How tall are you?	Numbers in order within 180	40
Half price sale	Halving and doubling money	42
Tables stars	Tables facts within 36	44
Ice pops	Multiples of 5 and 10; negative numbers	46
More tables stars	Tables facts within 36	48
Speedy tables	Mental recall of tables facts	50
Keeping fit	Addition and subtraction within 100	52
Six times table	Six times table	54
Multiplying	Multiplication within 100	56
What's missing?	Missing numbers and operations	58
Dividing marbles	Dividing by 2 within 100	60
More dividing	Dividing by 2 within 100	62
Nines and tens	Addition and subtraction within 100	64
Make one hundred	Addition to 100	66

Counting and place value

Addition and subtraction

Multiplication and division

Mixed problems

This is one hundred ... and this is one hundred.

How many is this?

132

1 How many is this?

3 How many?

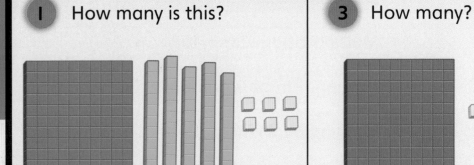

2 How many?

4 How many?

Work with a partner.

Make each number with one hundred, tens and ones.

I'll check your number.

Yes, that's 153.

Then draw it.

153

Make each number then draw it.

5 147

8 120

11 124

14 170

6 102

9 111

12 136

15 155

7 179

10 157

13 168

16 108

17 One hundred and forty-three

18 One hundred and fifty

How tall are you?

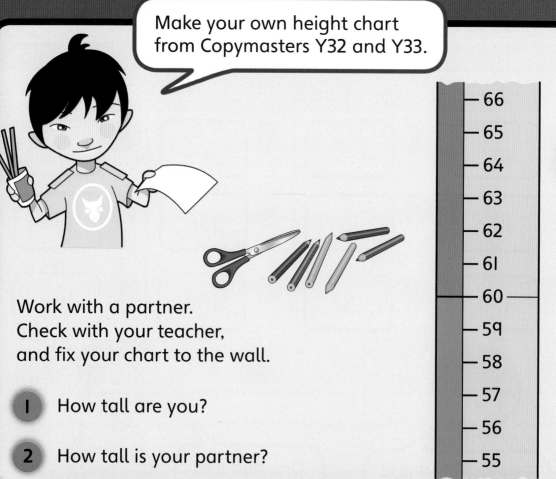

Work with a partner.
Check with your teacher,
and fix your chart to the wall.

1   How tall are you?

2   How tall is your partner?

Use your height chart, or do these in your head.

3 I'm 134 cm tall.
I'm 10 cm taller than you. How tall am I?

4 I'm 151 cm tall.
I'm 2 cm shorter than you. How tall am I?

5 I'm 160 cm tall.
I'm 4 cm shorter. How tall am I?

6 I'm 145 cm tall.
I'm 9 cm taller. How tall am I?

7 Who is taller, you or your partner?

8 How much taller?

Numbers in order within 180
Copymasters Y32 and Y33

Half price sale

Everything is half price in this sale!

£7.00 £3.50

How much do these cost in the sale?

1

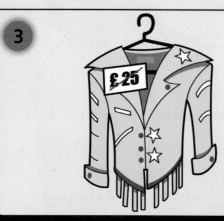

£12.00

2

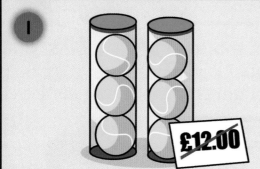

£9.00

3

£25

4

£6.50

5

£11.00

6

£1.50

This was half price!
It cost me £3.

So it cost £6
<u>before</u> the sale.

How much did these cost, <u>before</u> the sale?

7

£8.00

10

£7.50

8

£12.00

11

£1.30

9

£1.25

12
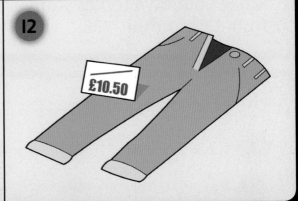
£10.50

Ask if you can play the 'Half price sale' game.

Halving and doubling money
Copymasters Y34 and Y35
The 'Half price sale' gale (Y58 and Y59)

Tables stars

I use these tables stars to practise my tables.

What is 3 times 4?

3 rows of 4 stars ... $3 \times 4 = 12$.

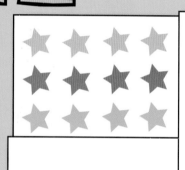

Tables stars

Make your own tables stars from Copymaster Y36.

Use your tables stars.

1	2×5	**4**	4×4	**7**	5×3
2	5×4	**5**	6×3	**8**	5×5
3	3×3	**6**	2×6	**9**	6×6

A game for 2 people.
You need: two 1 to 6 dice
and the tables stars cards.

Practise your tables like this.
Throw the dice.
Multiply the numbers.

2 times 4 is 8

Your partner checks
with the tables stars
like this.

Yes, 2 × 4 is 8.

Tables
stars

Tables
stars

Have ten turns each ... or more!

Ice pops

These ice pops are 10p each. How much for 2?

2 times 10p. That's 20p.

These ice pops are 10p each. How much for:

1. 3 ice pops?
2. 5 ice pops?
3. 9 ice pops?
4. 10 ice pops?

5. 12 ice pops?
6. 15 ice pops?
7. 17 ice pops?
8. 20 ice pops?

These ice pops are 5p each. How much for:

9. 5 ice pops?
10. 7 ice pops?
11. 8 ice pops?

12. 11 ice pops?
13. 9 ice pops?
14. 14 ice pops?

15. How many ice pops for 30p?

16. How many for £1.00?

20 ice pops in a box.

How many in:

17 2 boxes? **18** 4 boxes? **19** 5 boxes?

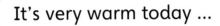

It's very warm today ...

but it's cold in the ice box of the fridge.

20 What is the temperature?

21 What is the temperature?

22 What is the temperature in your classroom today?

Multiples of 5 and 10: negative numbers
Copymasters Y38, Y39 and Y40

More tables stars

Use tables stars cards made from Copymaster Y36.

Use tables stars to practise dividing.

What is 15 divided by 3?

How many 3s make 15?

4 lots of 3 is not enough.

12

It's 5 lots of 3.

$15 \div 3 = 5$

Tabl... stars

Tabl... stars

Use your tables stars.

1	$12 \div 3$		5	$24 \div 6$		9	$12 \div 4$
2	$12 \div 2$		6	$20 \div 4$		10	$16 \div 4$
3	$15 \div 5$		7	$9 \div 3$		11	$6 \div 2$
4	$30 \div 6$		8	$24 \div 4$		12	$36 \div 6$

Tables facts within 36

Do these in your head.
Then check with your tables stars.

13 How many 5s make 20?

14 How many 3s make 18?

15 How many 4s make 24?

This is another way of writing a division.

How many 3s in 12?

$$3 \overline{)12}$$

$$3 \overline{)\,12}^{\,4}$$

You write the answer on top of the line.

Leave enough space for the answer when you write the question!

Copy and complete.

16 $2 \overline{)10}$

17 $3 \overline{)15}$

18 $5 \overline{)25}$

19 $2 \overline{)12}$

20 $3 \overline{)18}$

21 $4 \overline{)16}$

Speedy tables

> Work with a partner.

Write question numbers 1 to 20.
Ask your partner to read the questions to you.

> Write your answers as quickly as you can.

1	3 × 4	**8**	16 ÷ 4	**15**	3 × 8
2	2 × 7	**9**	80 ÷ 10	**16**	18 ÷ 2
3	0 × 5	**10**	15 ÷ 3	**17**	8 × 5
4	1 × 8	**11**	21 ÷ 3	**18**	45 ÷ 5
5	10 × 6	**12**	32 ÷ 4	**19**	4 × 9
6	5 × 4	**13**	30 ÷ 3	**20**	25 ÷ 5
7	6 × 2	**14**	30 ÷ 5		

✔ or ✗

> Now <u>you</u> read the questions to your partner.

How many 3s make 21?

3s into 21 ... that's 7.

21	$10 \div 2$		**24**	$35 \div 5$		**27**	$18 \div 3$
22	$12 \div 3$		**25**	$40 \div 10$		**28**	$28 \div 4$
23	$24 \div 4$		**26**	$8 \div 8$		**29**	$16 \div 2$

Copy and complete.

30 $\square \times 4 = 16$

31 $3 \times \square = 9$

32 $1 \times \square = 1$

33 $\square \times 9 = 27$

34 $10 \times \square = 100$

35 $\square \times 4 = 40$

Use a stopwatch or a sand timer.

Can you get 20 questions right in 3 minutes?

Use Speedy tables C made from Copymaster Y43.

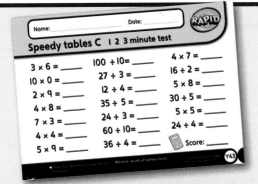

Check your answers. ✔ or ✘
Count how many you got right.

Ask what to do next.

Keeping fit

I want to do 100 skips a day!

I did 43 this morning, and 48 this afternoon.

1 How many skips altogether?

2 How many more skips, to make 100?

I did 55 this morning, and 40 this afternoon.

3 How many skips altogether?

4 How many more skips, to make 100?

I kept a chart for a week.

<u>Skipping</u>
Monday   43 + 50 =
Tuesday   45 + 55 =
Wednesday 70 + 30 =
Thursday   58 + 38 =
Friday   29 + 61 =
Saturday   50 + 50 =
Sunday   25 + 65 =

5 Copy and complete the chart.

6 On which days did I do 100 skips?

I ride my bike round a track. I keep a list each week.

7 How many laps altogether, in the 1st week?

Hint
Look for tens to help you add these in your head.

Laps on my bike
1st week
Mon. 4   Fri. 6
Tues. 4   Sat. 6
Wed. 5   Sun. 7
Thurs. 5

8 How many laps altogether, in the 2nd week?

Hint
Add the tens first, to help you add these in your head.

Laps on my bike
2nd week
Mon. 10   Fri. 12
Tues. 11   Sat. 14
Wed. 10   Sun. 10
Thurs. 10

9 How many laps altogether, in the 3rd week?

Laps on my bike
3rd week
Mon. 12   Fri. 18
Tues. 12   Sat. 12
Wed. 13   Sun. 10
Thurs. 12

Add in your head if you can.

 ✔ or ✘

Six times table

0, 6, 12, 18, 24, 30, ...
These numbers are called <u>multiples of six</u>.

You can get <u>multiples of six</u> by adding sixes,
or by <u>multiplying</u> by six.

One beetle

1 How many legs?

2 | 1 | × | 6 | = |

Three beetles

3 How many legs?

4 6 + 6 + 6

5 | 3 | × | 6 | = |

Four beetles

6 How many legs?

7 6 + 6 + 6 + 6

8 | 4 | × | 6 | = |

Six beetles

9 How many legs?

10 6 + 6 + 6 + 6 + 6 + 6

11 | 6 | × | 6 | = |

Seven beetles

12 How many legs?

13 6 + 6 + 6 + 6 + 6 + 6 + 6

14 ☐7☐ × ☐6☐ = ☐

Eight beetles

15 How many legs?

16 6 + 6 + 6 + 6 + 6 + 6 + 6 + 6

17 ☐8☐ × ☐6☐ = ☐

Fifty-four legs

18 How many beetles?

19 6 + 6 + 6 + 6 + 6 + 6 + 6 + 6 + 6

20 ☐9☐ × ☐6☐ = ☐

21 Copy and complete.

Six times table

0 × 6 =	4 × 6 =	8 × 6 =
1 × 6 =	5 × 6 =	9 × 6 =
2 × 6 =	6 × 6 =	10 × 6 =
3 × 6 =	7 × 6 =	

Six times table
Copymasters Y46 and Y47

Multiplying

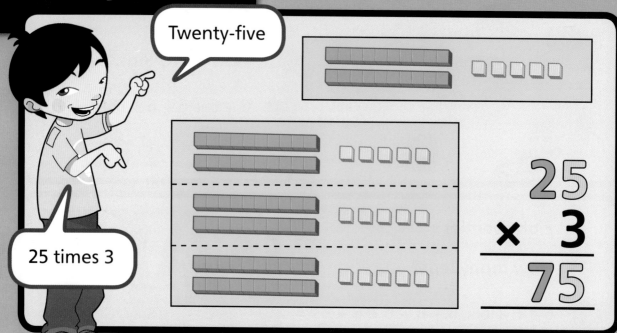

Twenty-five

25 times 3

$$25 \times 3 = 75$$

Make 3 lots of each number
with tens and ones.

Copy and complete.

Seventeen	1 $\begin{array}{r} {}^2\ 17 \\ \times\ \ 3 \\ \hline \end{array}$
Twenty-six	2 $\begin{array}{r} 26 \\ \times\ \ 3 \\ \hline \end{array}$
Twenty-eight	3 $\begin{array}{r} 28 \\ \times\ \ 3 \\ \hline \end{array}$
Thirty-three	4 $\begin{array}{r} 33 \\ \times\ \ 3 \\ \hline \end{array}$

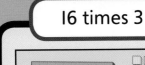

16 times 3	16 times 4	16 times 5

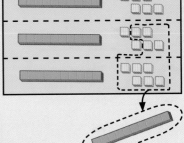 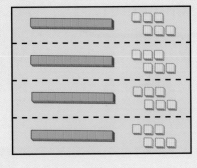 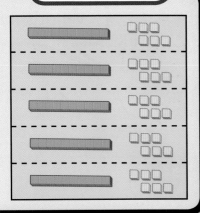

Copy and complete.

5
$$\begin{array}{r} 16 \\ \times\ \ 3 \\ \hline \\ \hline \end{array}$$

6
$$\begin{array}{r} 16 \\ \times\ \ 4 \\ \hline \\ \hline \end{array}$$

7
$$\begin{array}{r} 16 \\ \times\ \ 5 \\ \hline \\ \hline \end{array}$$

Use tens and ones.
Then multiply on paper.

$$\begin{array}{r} 25 \\ \times\ 3 \\ \hline 60 \quad (20 \times 3) \\ 15 \quad (5 \times 3) \\ \hline 75 \end{array}$$

8
$$\begin{array}{r} 21 \\ \times\ \ 2 \\ \hline \\ \hline \end{array}$$

10
$$\begin{array}{r} 22 \\ \times\ \ 4 \\ \hline \\ \hline \end{array}$$

12
$$\begin{array}{r} 18 \\ \times\ \ 4 \\ \hline \\ \hline \end{array}$$

14
$$\begin{array}{r} 29 \\ \times\ \ 2 \\ \hline \\ \hline \end{array}$$

9
$$\begin{array}{r} 29 \\ \times\ \ 3 \\ \hline \\ \hline \end{array}$$

11
$$\begin{array}{r} 20 \\ \times\ \ 5 \\ \hline \\ \hline \end{array}$$

13
$$\begin{array}{r} 13 \\ \times\ \ 5 \\ \hline \\ \hline \end{array}$$

15
$$\begin{array}{r} 47 \\ \times\ \ 2 \\ \hline \\ \hline \end{array}$$

What's missing?

What's missing here?

2 + ☐ = 5

3 Three.

Check

What's missing?

1. 1 4 + ☐ = 2 0
2. 9 − ☐ = 5
3. ☐ + 3 0 = 3 9
4. ☐ − 4 = 4

What's missing here?

4 ☐ 2 = 6

Add. **+**

5. 2 ☐ 8 = 1 0
6. 8 ☐ 5 = 3
7. 5 4 ☐ 4 = 5 0
8. 8 ☐ 8 = 1 6

Missing numbers and operations

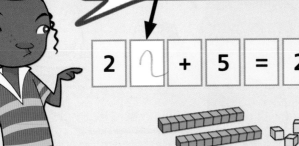

What's missing?

9. $3\,\boxed{} - 8 = 30$ 10. $\boxed{}\,4 + 6 = 40$

11. $1\,\boxed{} + 5 = 20$ 12. $\boxed{}\,2 - 30 = 2$

13. $48 - \boxed{} = 40$ 14. $2\,\boxed{} - 20 = 5$

15.

What's missing here?

$2 \times 2 = 4$

Is there more than one answer?

Ask if you can play the 'What's missing?' game.

Missing numbers and operations
Copymasters Y50 and Y51 The 'What's missing?' game (Y60, Y61 and Y62)

59

Dividing marbles

These marbles come in bags of ten ... or in ones.

We'll share them between the two of us.

1 24 divided by 2

2 26 divided by 2

3 28 divided by 2

Copy and complete.

4 2)‾24‾ **5** 2)‾26‾ **6** 2)‾28‾

25 divided by 2

$$\frac{12\ r.\ 1}{2)\overline{25}}$$

Copy and complete.

7 2)‾20‾ **8** 2)‾21‾ **9** 2)‾22‾ **10** 2)‾23‾

11 44 divided by 2

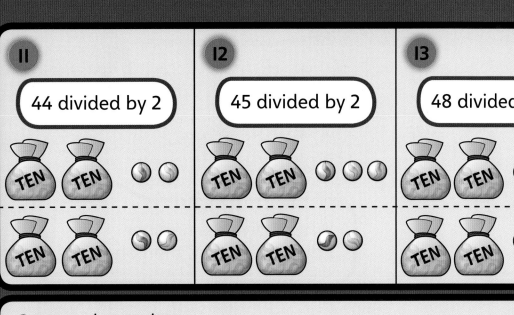

12 45 divided by 2

13 48 divided by 2

Copy and complete.

14 2) 44

15 2) 45

16 2) 48

32 marbles to share.

One bag of ten each.
We split the other bag of ten
into ones, so there are
12 ones to share.

16
2) 32

17 54 divided by 2

Copy and complete.

18 2) 54

19 2) 55

Dividing by 2 within 100
Copymasters Y52 and Y53

More dividing

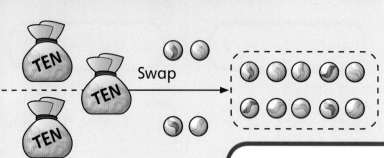

Swap

When I divide a number,
I divide tens first, then ones …

and sometimes
I split a ten into ten ones.

I can write it like this:

$$34 \div 2 = 17$$

or like this:

$$2\overline{)34}$$ = 17

Write your division both ways.

1 36 ÷ 2

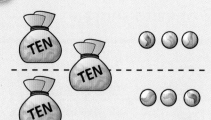

3 47 ÷ 2

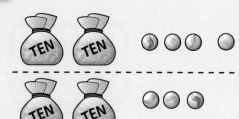

2 46 ÷ 2

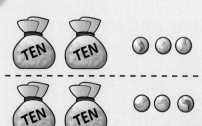

4 56 ÷ 2

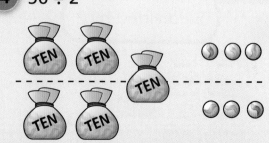

Dividing by 2 within 100

I'm using tens and ones. I can work this out in my head, like this:

$38 \div 2$

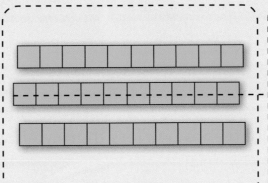

Half of 30 is 15

Half of 8 is 4

$$2\overline{)38} = 19$$

so half of 38 is 19.

Use tens and ones.

5 $2\overline{)32}$

6 $2\overline{)33}$

7 $2\overline{)42}$

8 $2\overline{)74}$

9 $2\overline{)83}$

10 $2\overline{)60}$

11 $2\overline{)88}$

12 $2\overline{)98}$

13 $2\overline{)75}$

14 $2\overline{)49}$

15 $2\overline{)57}$

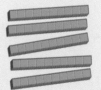

Dividing by 2 within 100
Copymasters Y54 and Y55

Nines and tens

1 How many here?

2 How many here?

Nineteen is <u>one less</u> than twenty.

If you want to add 19, you can add 20, then 'go back' one.

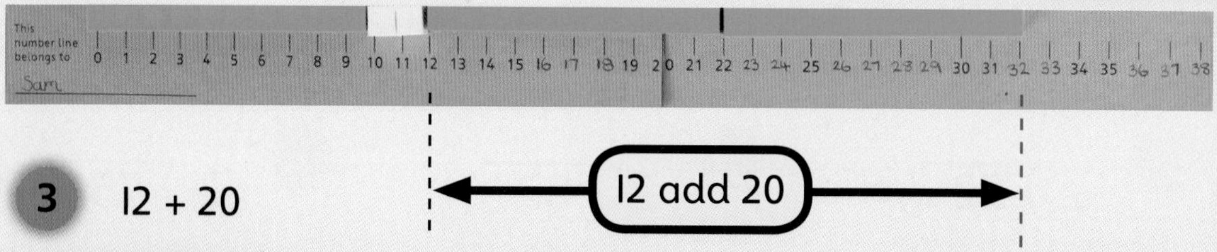

3 12 + 20

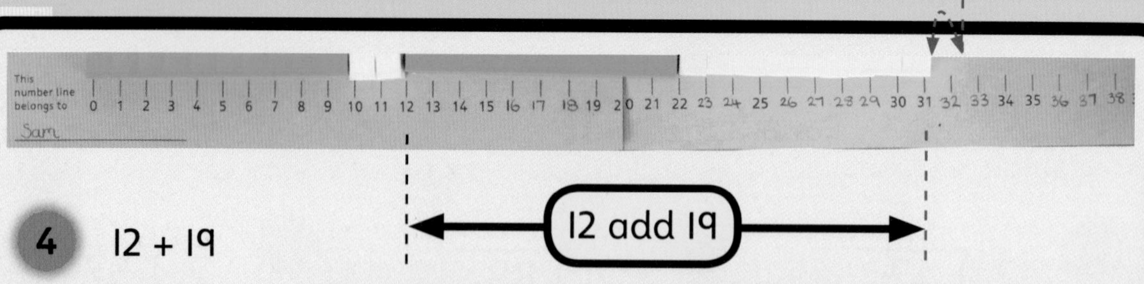

12 add 20

4 12 + 19

12 add 19

5 23 + 20	**7** 31 + 20	**9** 65 + 20
6 23 + 19	**8** 31 + 19	**10** 65 + 19

Do these in your head.

11	21 + 30	**14**	30 + 46	**17**	24 + 30
12	35 + 30	**15**	58 + 30	**18**	62 + 30
13	43 + 30	**16**	19 + 30	**19**	70 + 30

Do these with tens and ones.

20	21 + 29	**23**	29 + 46	**26**	24 + 29
21	35 + 29	**24**	58 + 29	**27**	62 + 29
22	43 + 29	**25**	19 + 29	**28**	70 + 29

Do these on paper.

$$\begin{array}{r} 41 \\ + 30 \\ \hline \end{array}$$

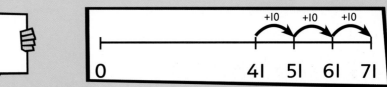

+10   +10   +10

0   41   51   61   71

29	76 + 20	**33**	68 + 20	**37**	56 + 30
30	76 + 19	**34**	68 + 19	**38**	56 + 29
31	37 + 20	**35**	41 + 30	**39**	29 + 30
32	37 + 19	**36**	41 + 29	**40**	29 + 29

Addition and subtraction within 100
Copymasters Y56 and Y57

Make one hundred

A game for 2 or 3 people.
You need: a calculator,
cards numbered 1 to 100,
10 tens and 10 ones.

Shuffle the cards.
Put them in a pile, face down.

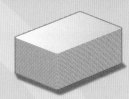

Take the top card.
Make that number with tens and ones.

Say how much more you would need
to make one hundred.

I need 68.

Check

$68 + 32 = 100$ ✔

You were right, so you keep the card.

Now it is your
partner's turn.

Have ten turns each ... or more!
Count how many cards you won.

Part 3
Contents

Two hundred	Counting to 200	68
Saving	Using money	70
Teen sums	Addition bonds to 16, 17 and 18	72
Halves	Halving within 120	74
Speedy tables	Mental recall of tables facts	76
Printing	Multiplication and division by 2 and 10	78
Sums to twenty	Addition and subtraction bonds within 20	80
Cheesecakes	Comparing $\frac{1}{2}$s, $\frac{1}{3}$s, $\frac{1}{4}$s and $\frac{1}{5}$s	82
More printing	Multiplication and division by 3 within 120	84
Number cards	Addition and subtraction within 120	86
Guinea pig sums	Arithmetic within 80	88
Inches and halves	Using halves	90
Café	Using money	92
Halves and quarters	Using halves and quarters	94
Cubes in groups	Investigating divisibility by 2, 3, 4, 5 and 6	96

Counting and place value

Addition and subtraction

Multiplication and division

Mixed problems

80 add 90

That's 170 altogether.

 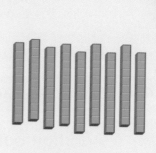

1 How many?

2 How many?

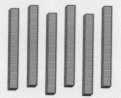 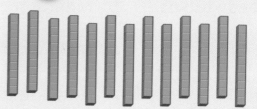

3 How many altogether?

4 How many?

5 How many?

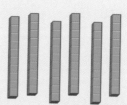

6 How many altogether?

7 How many?

8 How many?

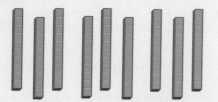 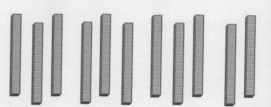

9 How many altogether?

Make 200

A game for 2 people.
You need: 3 hundreds,
20 tens and 20 ones and
two lots of cards numbered 1 to 9.

Shuffle the cards.
Put them in a pile, face down.

Take 2 cards.
Make the biggest
number you can.

Then collect that
many tens and ones.

Now it is your
partner's turn.

Keep taking turns.
Each time, count up how much you have altogether.

Swap when you can.

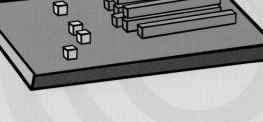

The winner is the first person to have 200 or more.

I'm saving for a poster.

MEGA POSTER £5

I've saved £3.60. How much more do I need?

£1.40

Use coins to check.

1

£2.20

I've saved £1.80. How much more do I need?

3

£4.99

I've saved £2.90. How much more do I need?

2

£5.50

100 Dance songs

I've saved £3.50. How much more do I need?

4

£8.00

I've saved £5.70. How much more do I need?

5

£16.50

I've saved £8.00.
How much more do I need?

7

£35.00

I've saved £17.00.
How much more do I need?

6

£48.00

I've saved £27.30.
How much more do I need?

8

£29.50

I've saved £19.75.
How much more do I need?

9

I saved 50p a week for 12 weeks.
How much did I save altogether?

I saved £3 a month for 6 months.
How much did I save altogether?

10

11 I saved £4 a month for 4 months.
How much did I save altogether?

Teen sums

How do _you_ work out 7 + 8?

Double 7 ... then add 1.

What is:

1 double 7? 14

2 double 7, add 1? 15

3 double 6? 12

4 double 6, add 1? 13

5 double 8? 16

6 double 8, add 1? 17

7 double 9? 18

8 double 9, add 1? 20

Do these in your head if you can.

9 6 + 6 11

10 7 + 7 14

11 8 + 8 16

12 9 + 9 18

13 8 + 9 17

14 6 + 7 13

15 10 + 9 19

16 7 + 8 15

17 7 + 6 13

18 9 + 10 19

19 8 + 7 15

20 9 + 8 17

Addition bonds to 16, 17 and 18

How do **you** work out 7 + 8?

7 add 3 makes 10 ... add 5 more.

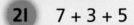

21	7 + 3 + 5	**26**	7 + 8
22	6 + 4 + 3	**27**	6 + 7
23	5 + 5 + 3	**28**	5 + 8
24	8 + 2 + 7	**29**	8 + 9
25	9 + 1 + 4	**30**	9 + 5

Do these sums make 16?

Write <u>Yes</u> or <u>No</u>.

31	4 + 5 + 6	**33**	2 + 8 + 6
32	7 + 6 + 3	**34**	4 + 4 + 8

Ask if you can play the 'Eighteens' game.

Addition bonds to 16, 17 and 18
Copymasters Y66 and Y67
The 'Eighteens' game (Y88 and Y89)

73

Halves

What's half of 48?

24

What is half of:

1 18?   3 90?   5 110?   7 66?

2 46?   4 94?   6 82?   8 120?

Answer these 'halves' questions.

9   How many eggs in half a dozen?

10 How many minutes in half an hour?

11 How many months in half a year?

MARCH

Now answer these.

12 What is half of £1?

13 What is half the number of legs on a spider?

14 What is half of 58 marbles?

15 Make up 3 or 4 'halves' questions.
    Give them to your partner to answer.   ✔ or ✘

I'm 5.

I'm 10.
You are half my age.

16 I'm 34.

I'm half her age.
How old am I?

17 I'm 28.

I'm half his age.
How old am I?

18 I'm 76.

I'm half her age.
How old am I?

19 How old are you?
Do you know anyone who is half <u>your</u> age?

20 I'm 12.
My brother is 6.
He is half my age.

Will my brother <u>always</u>
be half my age?

Halving within 120
Copymasters Y68 and Y69

Work with a partner.

Write question numbers 1 to 20.
Ask your partner to read the questions to you.

Write your answers
as quickly as you can.

1	3 × 10	**8**	70 ÷ 10	**15**	9 × 4
2	7 × 5	**9**	8 ÷ 2	**16**	6 ÷ 6
3	2 × 4	**10**	9 ÷ 3	**17**	9 × 5
4	6 × 3	**11**	6 ÷ 1	**18**	24 ÷ 6
5	9 × 2	**12**	25 ÷ 5	**19**	8 × 10
6	6 × 0	**13**	18 ÷ 2	**20**	30 ÷ 6
7	8 × 5	**14**	36 ÷ 4		

 ✔ or ✘

Now <u>you</u> read the questions to your partner.

Mental recall of tables facts

Copy and complete.

21 $\boxed{} \times 3 = 12$

22 $2 \times \boxed{} = 18$

23 $10 \times \boxed{} = 20$

24 $\boxed{} \times 1 = 5$

25 $6 \times \boxed{} = 36$

26 $\boxed{} \times 3 = 21$

How many 4s make 20?

4s into 20? That's 5.

27 $20 \div 4$

28 $8 \div 4$

29 $24 \div 4$

30 $4 \div 4$

31 $40 \div 4$

32 $28 \div 4$

33 $16 \div 4$

34 $12 \div 4$

35 $32 \div 4$

Use a stopwatch or a sand timer.

Use Speedy tables E made from Copymaster Y70.

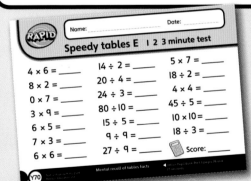

Name: _____ Date: _____

Speedy tables E 1 2 3 minute test

$4 \times 6 =$ _____ $14 \div 2 =$ _____ $5 \times 7 =$ _____
$8 \times 2 =$ _____ $20 \div 4 =$ _____ $18 \div 2 =$ _____
$0 \times 7 =$ _____ $24 \div 3 =$ _____ $4 \times 4 =$ _____
$3 \times 9 =$ _____ $80 \div 10 =$ _____ $45 \div 5 =$ _____
$6 \times 5 =$ _____ $15 \div 5 =$ _____ $10 \times 10 =$ _____
$7 \times 3 =$ _____ $9 \div 9 =$ _____ $18 \div 3 =$ _____
$6 \times 6 =$ _____ $27 \div 9 =$ _____   Score:

Mental recall of tables facts

Can you get 20 sums right in 3 minutes?

Check your answers. ✔ or ✘
Count how many you got right.

Ask what to do next.

Printing

2 lizards on a rubber stamp.

How many lizards when I print 4 times?

8

$$4 \times 2 = 8$$

How many lizards when I print ...

1. 7 times?
2. 9 times?
3. 13 times?
4. 26 times?

5. 22 times?
6. 35 times?
7. 41 times?
8. 38 times?
9. 54 times?
10. 60 times?

$$\begin{array}{r} 26 \\ \times\ 2 \\ \hline \end{array}$$

Multiplication and division by 2 and 10 within 120

32 lizards.
How many times did I print?

2s into 32 ... 16

11 38 lizards.
How many times did Jacob print?

12 54 lizards.
How many times did Jacob print?

13

68 lizards.
How many times did I print?

14 110 lizards!
How many times did Jacob print?

Sums to twenty

> I can do sums up to 15 in my head.

> Keep practising for sums up to 20.

$$7 + 7 = 14$$

$$9 + 6 = 15$$

$$8 + 9 = 17$$

$$14 - 8 = 6$$

$$20 - 8 = 12$$

$$14 + 5 = 19$$

Do these in your head.

1. $3 + 4$
2. $8 + 7$
3. $13 - 3$

4. $6 + 6$
5. $5 + 9$
6. $15 - 6$

7. $15 - 8$
8. $10 - 3$
9. $6 + 8$

Do these with tens and ones.

10. $5 + 14$
11. $13 - 6$
12. $7 + 11$
13. $12 - 4$

14. $13 + 7$
15. $2 + 16$
16. $9 - 0$
17. $20 - 5$

18. $11 + 8$
19. $19 - 13$
20. $20 - 8$
21. $9 + 8$

Do these on a number line.

22	8 + 6	**26**	20 − 9	**30**	10 + 8
23	12 + 7	**27**	16 − 13	**31**	3 + 16
24	4 + 15	**28**	18 − 5	**32**	9 + 9
25	14 + 6	**29**	19 − 14	**33**	17 + 2

Do each of these in your head, then check on a calculator.

34	9 + 4	**37**	16 − 7	**40**	8 + 9
35	8 + 8	**38**	17 − 3	**41**	12 + 6
36	16 + 4	**39**	19 − 10	**42**	3 + 14

Ask if you can play the 'Make 20' game.

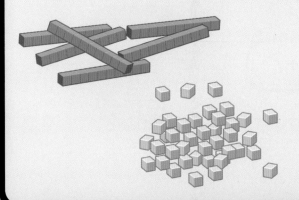
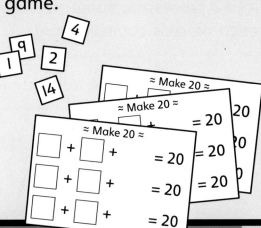

≈ Make 20 ≈

☐ + ☐ + ☐ = 20

☐ + ☐ + ☐ = 20

☐ + ☐ + ☐ = 20

Addition and subtraction bonds within 20
Copymaster Y73
The 'Make 20' game (Y90, Y91 and Y92)

Ⓖ

Cheesecakes

We're sharing this between 2.

$\frac{1}{2}$

$\frac{1}{2}$

If you cut something into 2 pieces <u>the same size</u>, each piece is called a <u>half</u>.

Is each piece $\frac{1}{2}$? Write <u>Yes</u> or <u>No</u>.

1

2

3

If you cut something into 3 pieces the same size, each piece is called a <u>third</u>.

We're in luck! $\frac{1}{3}$ each.

Is each piece $\frac{1}{3}$? Write <u>Yes</u> or <u>No</u>.

4 **5** **6**

If you cut something
into 4 pieces the same size,
each piece is called a <u>quarter</u>.

$\frac{1}{4}$ each.

Is each piece $\frac{1}{4}$? Write <u>Yes</u> or <u>No</u>.

7 **8** **q**

10 This is a <u>fifth</u> of a cheesecake.
How many pieces do you think
the cake was cut into?

$\frac{1}{5}$

3 kittens on a rubber stamp.

How many kittens when I print 3 times?

q

$3 \times 3 = 9$

How many kittens when I print …

1. 6 times?
2. 7 times?
3. 8 times?
4. 10 times?
5. 11 times?

6. 13 times?
7. 15 times?
8. 16 times?
9. 19 times?
10. 24 times?

$$\begin{array}{r} 13 \\ \times\ 3 \\ \hline \\ \hline \end{array}$$

Multiplication and division by 3 within 120
Copymasters Y76 and Y77

Number cards

Use number cards from 0 to 40 to practise adding and taking away.

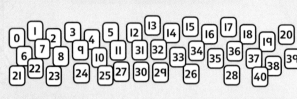

Take two cards.

| 14 | 25 |

Make up two sums.

$$\begin{array}{r} 25 \\ + 14 \\ \hline 39 \end{array} \qquad \begin{array}{r} 25 \\ - 14 \\ \hline 11 \end{array}$$

Add these.

1 6 28   **3** 17 16   **5** 36 34   **7** 24 30

2 13 22   **4** 26 5   **6** 3 15   **8** 18 33

Take away.

Check. ✔ or ✘

9 40 14   **11** 23 9   **13** 19 0

10 29 7   **12** 20 4   **14** 31 8

choose 2 numbers

A game for 2 people.
You need: a calculator, and cards numbered 0 to 40.

Shuffle the cards.
Put them in a pile, face down.
Take the top 4 cards and lay them in a line.

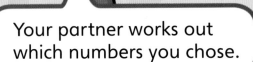

| 5 | 25 | 33 | 36 |

Secretly choose 2 numbers. Add them up.

Your partner works out which numbers you chose.

25 and 33

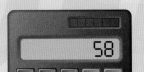

58

If your partner is right, they can take the 2 cards and keep them.

Put 2 more cards in the line to make 4 again.

Now it is your partner's turn.

Have 6 turns each ... or more!

Addition and subtraction within 120
Copymasters Y78 and Y79

Guinea pig sums

Guinea pigs have 4 toes on their front feet ...
and 3 toes on their back feet.

4 toes

3 toes

1 How many toes on a guinea pig, altogether?

2 How many toes on 2 guinea pigs?

3 How many toes on 3 guinea pigs?

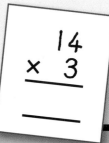

$$\begin{array}{r} 14 \\ \times\ \ 3 \\ \hline \end{array}$$

70 toes

4 How many guinea pigs?

5 How many toes on 4 guinea pigs?

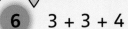 These sums just use 3s and 4s.

6 3 + 3 + 4

7 4 + 3 + 4

8 4 + 4 + 4

9 3 + 3 + 3 + 3

10 3 + 4 + 4 + 4

11 4 + 3 + 4 + 3 + 4

12 4 + 4 + 4 + 3 + 3 + 3

13 3 + 3 + 4 + 3 + 3

14 4 + 4 + 4 + 4 + 3

15 3 + 3 + 3 + 4 + 3 + 3

16 Write a sum with 3s and 4s which makes 14.

17 Write a sum with 3s and 4s which makes 22.

18 Write a sum with 3s and 4s which makes 25.

Inches and halves

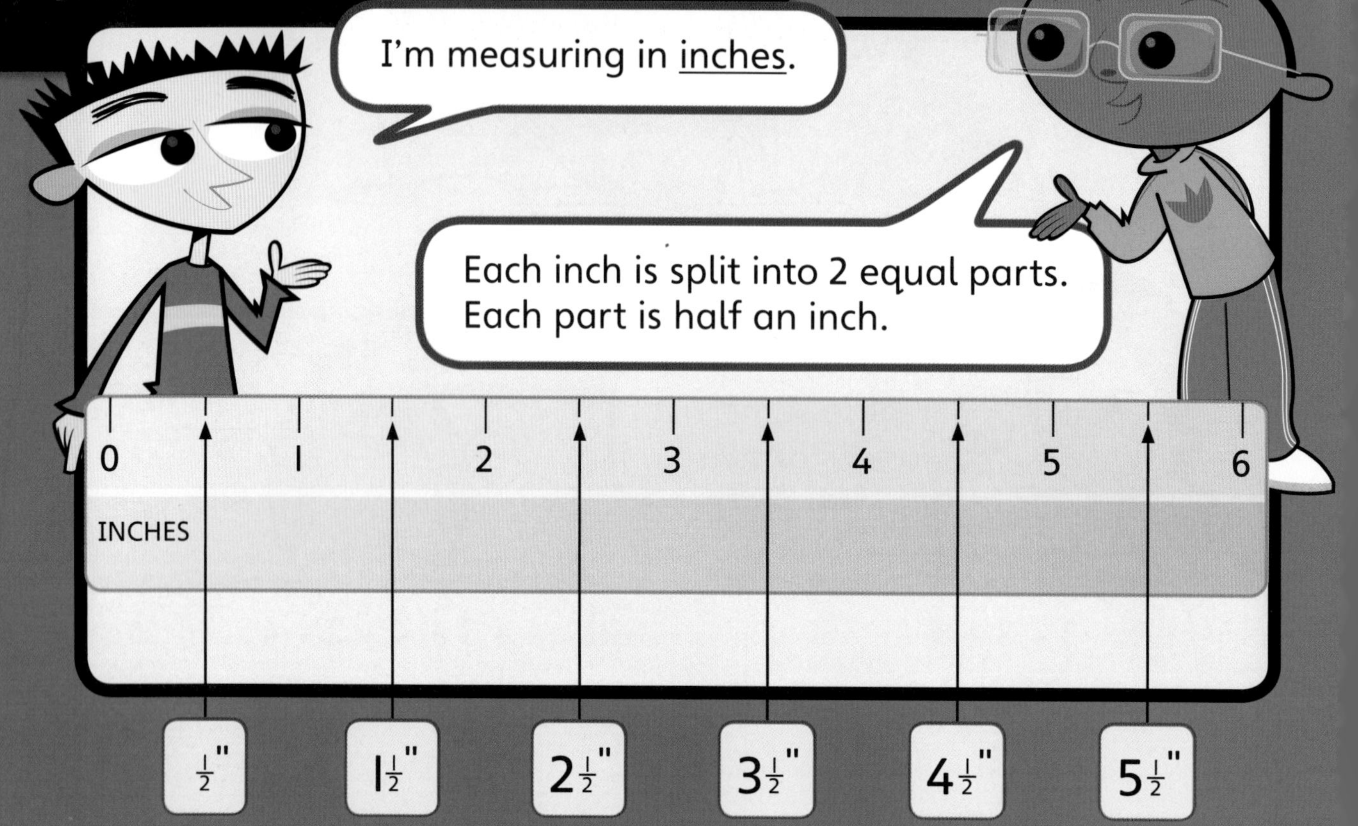

I'm measuring in <u>inches</u>.

Each inch is split into 2 equal parts.
Each part is half an inch.

0   1   2   3   4   5   6

INCHES

$\frac{1}{2}$" $1\frac{1}{2}$" $2\frac{1}{2}$" $3\frac{1}{2}$" $4\frac{1}{2}$" $5\frac{1}{2}$"

How tall is each penguin?

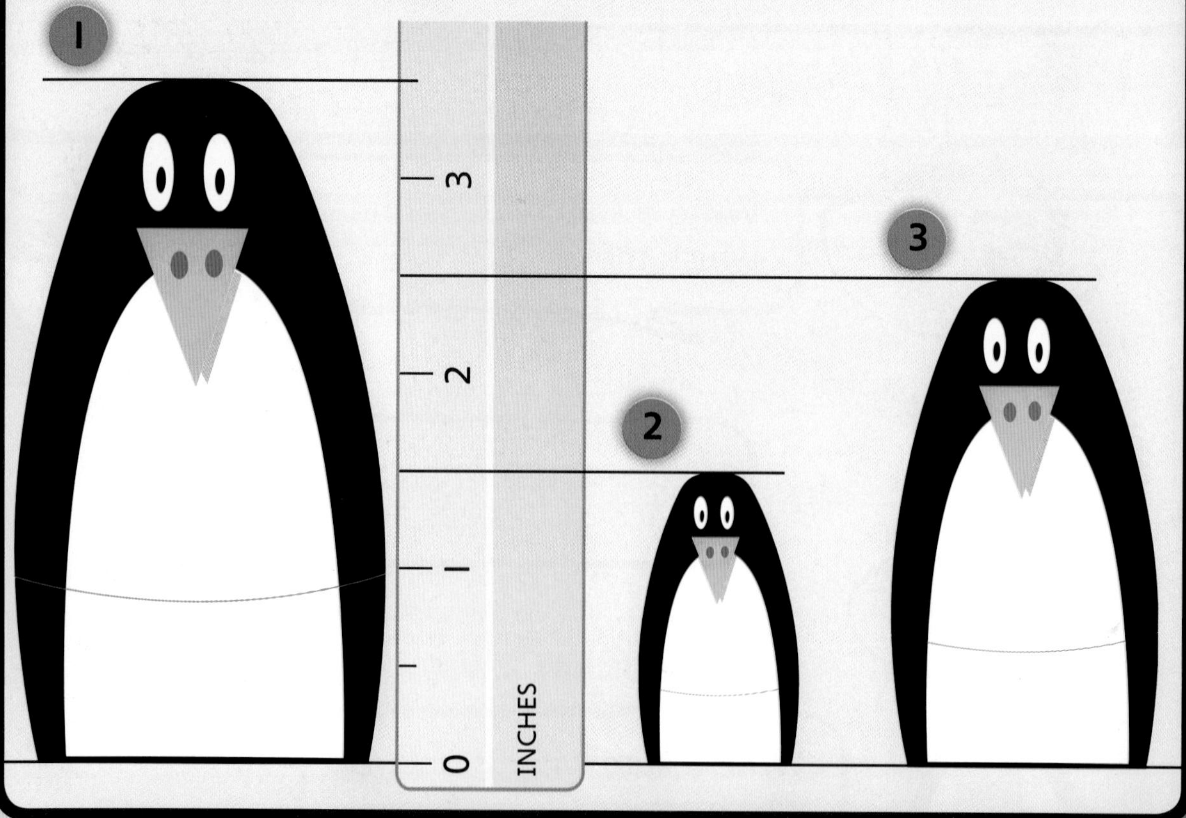

1

2

3

3

2

1

0

INCHES

How long is each fish? Measure to the nearest $\frac{1}{2}$".

4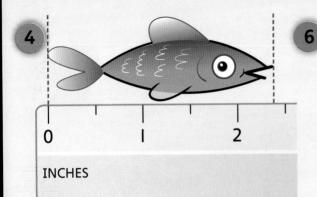

0   1   2

INCHES

6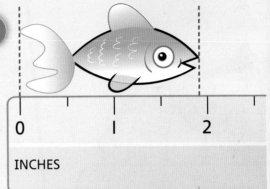

0   1   2

INCHES

5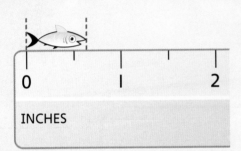

0   1   2

INCHES

7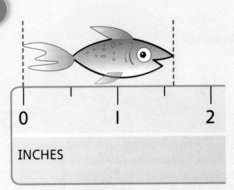

0   1   2

INCHES

Can you count in halves?

$\frac{1}{2}$, 1, 1$\frac{1}{2}$, 2, 2$\frac{1}{2}$, 3, ...

Copy and complete.

8 2, 2$\frac{1}{2}$, 3, ___, 4, 4$\frac{1}{2}$, ___, ___.

9 5, 5$\frac{1}{2}$, ___, 6$\frac{1}{2}$, 7, ___, ___.

10 7, 7$\frac{1}{2}$, 8, ___, 9, ___, 10, ___, ___.

Using halves
Copymasters Y82 and Y83

Café

★ Corner ★ Cafe ★

£1.40 — TOASTED SANDWICH

70p — MONSTER MUFFIN

CRISPS — 30p — CRISPS

60p — TEA

70p — COFFEE

80p — HOT CHOCOLATE

60p — CANS

STRAWBERRY BANANA CHOCOLATE — MILKSHAKES — 90p

> I bought a strawberry milkshake.
> It cost 90p.

1

> What flavour milkshake would <u>you</u> choose?

How much for these?

2 Monster muffin, please.

3 Hot chocolate, please.

4 Can of cola, please.

5 Toasted sandwich, please.

6 Crisps, please.

7 Tea, please.

Halves and quarters

How much cheesecake is on each plate?

one quarter

two quarters

three quarters

$\frac{1}{4}$

$\frac{2}{4}$

$\frac{3}{4}$

How much cheesecake is on each plate?

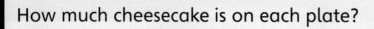

I've got half a cheesecake.

I've got two quarters.

$\frac{1}{2}$  $\frac{2}{4}$

5 Who has the most?

6 Which is bigger, half a cheesecake or three quarters of a cheesecake?

I'm measuring in <u>inches</u>.

Each inch is split into 4 equal parts. Each part is quarter of an inch.

INCHES

0   1   2   3   4   5   6

$\frac{1}{4}$"

$\frac{1}{2}$"

$\frac{3}{4}$"

1"

$1\frac{1}{4}$"

$1\frac{1}{2}$"

$1\frac{3}{4}$"

2"

Half an inch is the same as two quarters of an inch.

How tall is each toy? Measure to the nearest $\frac{1}{4}$".

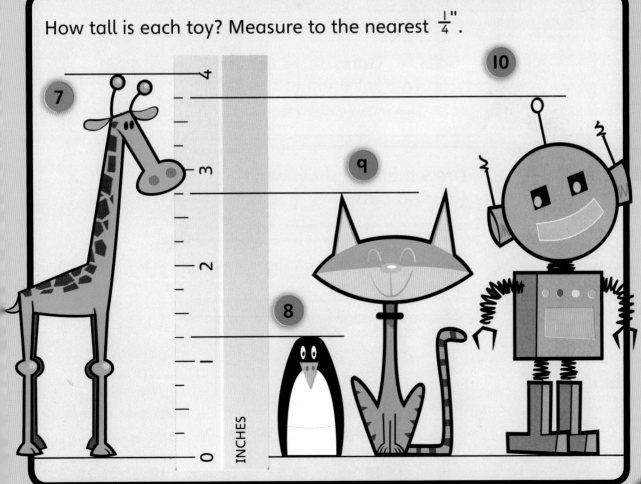

7

8

9

10

INCHES

Using halves and quarters
Copymasters Y86 and Y87

I can put 8 cubes in groups of 2 exactly ... but <u>not</u> in groups of 3.

I can put them in 4s but <u>not</u> 5s and not 6s.

1 Use 12 cubes. Can you put them in 2s, 3s, 4s, 5s and 6s?

Draw them, to show what you find out.

2 Now try again using 13 cubes.

3 Choose one of these numbers to try.

14 15 16 17 18 19 20